Around Henley-on-Thames

IN OLD PHOTOGRAPHS

Around Henley-on-Thames

IN OLD PHOTOGRAPHS

Collected by SIÂN ELLIS

A Budding Book

First published in 1992 by Alan Sutton Publishing Limited

This edition published in 1998 by Budding Books, an imprint of Sutton Publishing Limited
Phoenix Mill · Thrupp · Stroud · Gloucestershire
GL5 2BU

A catalogue record for this book is available from the British Library

ISBN 1-84015-070-X

Typesetting and origination by
Sutton Publishing Limited.
Printed in Great Britain by
WBC Limited, Bridgend, Mid-Glamorgan.

Contents

Introduction

When the idea of compiling a volume of old pictures of Henley and its surrounding area was raised, several people said to me, 'Henley residents will be too blasé, they won't be interested. They have their Royal Regatta, their fine houses and town which attract visitors by the thousand. They know they live in a highly desirable part of the country. It would be *just another book*.' A month later, after the *Henley Standard* had run a short piece on my project and asked readers to contact me, I was receiving letters daily from people with memories and pictures to share. One letter in particular, from Mrs Florence Povey, summed up the warmth with which an album of pictures might be greeted: 'It will bring back a lot of old memories of when I was young [in the 1920s] and the world seemed at peace, when everybody helped each other and children were safe to go into the woods and play like my brothers and I did.'

Such great affection for the past and for what has been lost to the modern age was echoed in every quarter. (There were, of course, acknowledgements of positive modern progress – we cannot be entirely dewy-eyed about years gone by!) The colourful and sometimes curious shops, now displaced by the supermarket, were a favourite topic. Some of these, such as Stanley Mead's, Duke Street (p. 34) – a shop which it must have been an adventure to go into – are collected here. Other tradesmen around Henley are recalled only by those with long memories, or could not be squeezed into the book due to lack of space: the muffin man who walked along the roads at Shiplake ringing a handbell, a tray of muffins on his head; or 'the midnight baker', Arthur Lambourne, who was renowned for delivering his bread late at night around Stoke Row, Checkendon, Woodcote and Sonning Common.

Many 'characters' were also fondly remembered: the Nettlebed sisters who ran a shopping service to Henley and Wallingford (p. 134); white-bearded 'Joe the Tramp', who would come into Henley with his begging tin, to be treated by one lady to tea carried out to him on a silver tray (others simply gave him pieces of cake); or the erstwhile carrier between Nettlebed and Reading who had a reputation for 'boozing'. While he was taking refreshment at Highmoor some of the local lads turned his horse to face in the wrong direction. When the carrier eventually emerged from the pub he was oblivious to his disorientation, but his trusty horse was more aware and faithfully trotted the right way home to Nettlebed. One wonders if the carrier was needed at all; the horse could have made the deliveries on its own. The Regatta produced many stories, of course, of gypsies sitting under the trees and telling fortunes, of punts being loaded with hampers and china crockery, and of the camaraderie of the crowds on the river.

Many hours were passed in animated discussion and many tales told during my visits to interested residents and I am indebted to all those, named in the Acknowledgements, who gave so freely of their time and hospitality to help me with my research. Perhaps one day all the information and anecdotes they gave me will fill a second book! But the present volume is concerned with pictures. It is not a general history of Henley and its surrounds: other books cover Henley from its days as a medieval market town and river port, and its coaching and wagon traffic in the eighteenth and nineteenth centuries, to its popularity as a tourist destination and commuter town. This is an album and the photographs tell their own stories of the last hundred or so years. And hopefully, like the pieces in a jigsaw, the captured glimpses fit together to convey a larger picture.

Many of the photographs come from individuals' personal collections and albums which, if they were not published here, might never have a wider audience than the owners' immediate family circles. They give to certain sections of the book a highly personal flavour, but such normally hidden pictures provide a more intimate insight into lives led in years gone by than professional images do. So it has been an aim of the book to blend professional and amateur, public and private views. I only wish I had not had to make so many agonizing choices over which pictures to leave out. Other photographs – many of the best quality ones – have come from the fascinating Oxfordshire Photographic Archive housed in the Centre for Oxfordshire Studies at the Central Library, Oxford. Anyone interested in old photographs of their area should certainly visit the collection.

The chapters which follow have been arranged partly as a result of the material available and partly with the idea of a tour in mind: beginning with Henley itself, over to Hambleden, back to Shiplake, Stoke Row and Nettlebed, and finally from Mapledurham to Goring. Each section is prefaced with a brief introduction which merely sets the scene. There are a few pictures for which information supplied is not complete or where specific dates have not been given (and in some instances where dates have been indicated, there has been lively debate about how exact one can be). If the pictures rouse memories which can provide further information, then that is as much the purpose of this book as the provision of answers and enjoyment. In any research, there is always more to be done.

Siân Ellis, 1992

SECTION ONE

Jolly Boating Weather

'This meeting is of the opinion that the establishing of an annual Regatta, under judicious and respectable management, would not only be productive of the most beneficial results to the town of Henley, but from its peculiar attractions would also be a source of amusement and gratification to the neighbourhood, and the public in general.'

This proposal, made at a public meeting in the Town Hall on 26 March 1839, launched the Henley Regatta. There was no great tradition of rowing at Henley, but the first Boat Race between Oxford and Cambridge Universities in 1829 had been rowed over the Henley Reach, attracting a good number of visitors and supporters to the town, much to the delight of local tradesmen, shopkeepers and innkeepers. Enthusiasm for some sort of annual rowing event grew with further races at Henley in 1831 (Oxford vs Leander Club) and 1837 (Lady Margaret Boat Club, Cambridge vs Queen's, Oxford), with the conclusion quoted above.

Although the Regatta, in conjunction with a fair and other attractions, was first promoted as a source of amusement for the local population and of trade for local business, its purpose as a venue for competitive amateur rowing soon came to the fore. Of course, not everyone appreciated the finer points of 'the blade on the feather' during 'jolly boating weather' rejoiced over in the 'Eton Boating Song'; many went (and go) to Henley as part of the social round. Indeed, since the Regatta came under royal patronage in 1851, it has been an established social fixture. However, the standard of rowing at Henley and the ever increasing number of entrants prove that whatever the spectators go to the races for, the sportsmen have their eyes set on trophies. Originally completed on one afternoon and consisting of two events – the Grand Challenge Cup and the Town Challenge Cup – the Regatta now extends over five days to accommodate fifteen events. Successive committees and stewards have achieved a remarkable record in steering the Regatta on a continuous course, interrupted only by the First and Second World Wars.

Every inhabitant of Henley, past and present, has favourite memories of the Regatta in years gone by. Mrs Hilda Austin remembers how she and her brothers would sleep in the shed of their Greys Road home so that their mother could take in more bed and breakfast guests during the Regatta in the 1930s and '40s. Perhaps more memories will be stirred by the pictures which follow.

The Grand, 1887. Of all the Challenge Trophies competed for at Henley Royal Regatta, the most prestigious remains the Grand Challenge Cup for eights, which dates from 1839, the first year of the Regatta. In that first year the 100 guinea cup was contested by four crews: Brasenose, Wadham and Oxford Etonians, with Cambridge University represented by Trinity. Accounts of the day suggest there was a huge amount of excitement in the town, despite unfortunate weather conditions of thunder, lightning and rain. Spectators poured in by stage coach or rowed in from London, Oxford and the shires. Not for nothing had the Regatta committee shrewdly published notices to regulate the crush: boats and barges were to take up stations only where the guard boats indicated, and 'All Horsemen are also requested to abstain from riding on the towing path during the day (the Umpire excepted)'! The Etonian Club of Oxford beat Brasenose in the first heat by about six lengths, and Trinity beat Wadham in the second heat. In the final, rowed in the early evening, Trinity won by half a length, having completed the mile and a half course from Temple Island to the Bridge in approximately eight minutes and thirty seconds.

The finish. By the time this picture was taken the Regatta finish had moved downstream from its original point at the Bridge. It was first moved in 1840, to the Red Lion lawn, to avoid the dangers of the Bridge, and then further moved in 1886 to Poplar Point, where the course finishes today. The start has also moved twice, first in 1886 to the bottom of Temple Island on the Bucks side of the river and then to the top of Temple Island in 1923/4. Each move was undertaken to make the course fairer and safer. This particular picture must date from some time around the beginning of the century, since the booming introduced in 1899 to keep riverborne spectators back from the course is visible. The increased orderliness of spectators' boats can be compared with the view on the opposite page, although the crowds of 1887 seem to have been remarkably well behaved despite the absence of booming. Nowadays, of course, spectators tend to watch races from the banks and hospitality tents, rather than take to the river in the droves of yesteryear.

Some of the crews. Above: The Leander crew opposite Hobbs' boathouse, 1890s. Leander Club is Britain's oldest rowing club, with a history which can be traced back to 1818. Although Leander did not enter a crew for the first Henley Regatta, a team did rather ostentatiously row with each heat – to demonstrate its superiority. The following year Leander actually entered the Grand Challenge Cup in the orthodox manner (the disgruntled stewards had ruled after the previous performance that no boat was to accompany races except that of the umpire) and it won. Leander's fortunes at Henley might have fluctuated over the years, but it remains an extremely successful and prestigious club.

Opposite:
The Eton crew after the Ladies' Challenge Plate, July 1902. The Ladies' Plate was first contested in 1845 and entries were restricted to university college crews and British schools. Only in 1968 was it opened to a wider field. Eton has a remarkable record of success at Henley and has notched up many more wins than any other British school.

Magdalen College IV, Oxford relaxing in June 1896. Oxford and Cambridge University crews were the lifeblood of the Regatta during its first century. Throughout that time the route to Henley was most usually via public school and Oxbridge rowing, and even Leander and other London clubs relied considerably on rowers from these channels to fill their boats. These days the sport is not confined to the privileged few, yet the traditional training grounds for the heroes of Henley retain their reputation.

Pennsylvania win a heat, 1890s. No sooner had overseas competitors begun to take part in Henley Regatta, in 1872, than the definition of amateur status was brought under the spotlight. In 1879 the Henley stewards declared that anyone who had competed for a stake or money, with or against professionals, taught or pursued athletic exercises as a means of gaining a livelihood, or been employed with boats, could not be an amateur. Moreover, 'Who is or has been, by trade or employment for wages, a mechanic, artisan, or labourer' could not compete. Despite the ruling, there were many contentious incidents, such as when a University of Pennsylvania crew reached the final of the Grand in 1901 – with a professional coach. But the inclusion of overseas crews, rather resisted by many in the early years, has made the Regatta a much richer event. So, too, has the removal in 1938 of the notorious 'manual labour ban' quoted above.

Man overboard! After being beaten by E.G. Hemmerde in the Diamond Skulls event in 1900, B.H. Howell collapsed and fell out of his boat. The lady in the foreground wielding a paddle seems afraid that her dog might follow suit! Another notable incident involving a competitor taking a dip occurred in 1868: the coxswain of the Brasenose College IV launched himself overboard in the first heat of the Stewards' Cup in order to lighten the boat's load. Brasenose won, but were disqualified. However, the incident helped precipitate the advent of the coxless fours, now an accepted attraction at the Regatta.

High-flying spectators. This photograph is believed to show the first aeroplane to fly over the Regatta. The year was 1914. It seems that some spectators will do anything to win the best view!

The Royal Grandstand, with Queen Mary. Henley Regatta became Royal in 1851 when Prince Albert accepted an invitation to become its patron, in place of Lord Camoys. Since the Prince Consort's agreement, every reigning British king or queen has reaffirmed the royal patronage. Prince Albert never actually attended the Regatta, but the Henley crowds were treated to a truly royal spectacle in 1887 when the fourth Lord Camoys brought a private party to the Regatta which included the Kings of Denmark and Greece, the Prince and Princess of Wales (later King Edward VII and Queen Alexandra) and their children. The next royal visit was that of King George V and Queen Mary in 1912, the first ever by a reigning British monarch. Henley resident Miss Sybil Reeves recalls the great excitement of seeing the royal couple arrive by train and then travel by royal barge to Greenlands to have lunch with Lord Hambleden. Sybil and her friends lined the river bank to wave flags and cheer – and to their huge delight the King raised his hat as the barge passed by.

Queen Mary presents prizes at the Regatta, 1912, watched by Princess Mary.

The Duke and Duchess of York visited the Regatta in 1931. For the duke it was a second visit; he had also attended in 1928.

Princesses Elizabeth and Margaret came to Henley in 1946. The occasion was marked by the naming of the new schools' trophy as the Princess Elizabeth Cup.

All dressed up. It was not just royalty who brought dignity and a sense of occasion to the Regatta, of course, as this civic group, seen some time around the 1920s, shows.

The social set aboard the houseboat *Stella*, 1890s. For many people the Regatta is as much an event on the social calendar as it is a sporting competition. Indeed, some people are reputed to have been to the Regatta without even seeing a race. During the nineteenth century houseboats succeeded barges as the principal craft for spectators, reaching a high-point at the turn of this century – and what beautifully decorated, luxurious floating mansions they were. One of the first large houseboats to make the journey to Henley was the *Athena* in around 1880. The dominance over the rowing of the social side to the Regatta was not lost on *Punch* magazine when it published 'A Regatta Rhyme', supposedly written on board the *Athena*, containing such memorable lines as: 'I love the fresh air, the lunch here and there, To see pretty toilettes and faces; But one thing I hate – allow me to state – The fuss they make over the Races.' But if the gentleman-author of the rhyme disliked the 'intrusion' of the rowing, many riparian owners were also upset by the sudden arrival of multitudes of houseboats at the bottom of their gardens to spoil their view. The problem was alleviated by a Thames Preservation Act in 1885, which empowered the Thames Conservancy to regulate the river traffic and where it could 'park'.

The houseboat *Folly*, *c*. 1899.

Picture postcard spectacle. The sight of many gloriously decorated houseboats lined up along the banks inevitably became the subject of postcards from Henley.

Water, water everywhere, but too many boats to see it. Spectators not on houseboats crammed the river with their rowing boats, skiffs and punts. This picture dates from around 1898.

A broader view of spectators 'messing about in boats', 1890s. The picture looks up towards Temple Island.

'River family', *c.* 1930. The river seems to run through the veins of some Henley families, and that is certainly the case as far as Mr Peter Sutherland, owner of the riverside Bird Place, Remenham, is concerned. Pictured here as a young lad (standing at the end of the punt), he grew up to become a captain of Leander and also founder of the Upper Thames Rowing Club. His father Douglas (front left) was the Hon. Treasurer of the Thames Punting Club. The picture also shows Peter's mother Ethel (front right) and his sisters Irene (middle) and Eugenie (back). Holding the camera was another sister, Phyllis, who subsequently became a Thames punting champion.

The Regatta provided a good occasion for family outings and snapshots. Spectators would tie their punts together and so form a platform over which anyone could walk when they wanted to reach the bank.

Set for the day. Once on the river, most spectators stayed there until the last race was rowed – which meant taking plenty of comfortable cushions and a picnic.

SECTION TWO

Business as Usual

To the outsider, Henley is synonymous with its Regatta. But for most of the year the town carries on its business as usual: not even Henley can escape the daily routine of work and school.

The beauty of the Henley area is that so much of historic interest is still clearly apparent. There is the attractive Georgian architecture of the town, for example, although this can mislead: in many cases it represents a 'modernization' of earlier structures which hide behind the façades. There are the former coaching inns, redolent of a flourishing eighteenth- and early nineteenth-century trade, before the advent of trains changed patterns of travel and closed an era.

Yet there is much which has vanished completely. Most obvious has been the disappearance of many colourful and idiosyncratic shops. In some instances the hollow shells of the buildings remain, but their fascinating owners have gone, and with them a magic which will never be recaptured. Where today would you find the intriguing variety of activities going on within the same business as in Stanley Mead's, once at 29 Duke Street (p. 34)? Can you imagine collecting a quarter of a hundredweight of coal in an old pram and wheeling it from the merchant's by the station all the way to Greys Road, as Mrs Hilda Austin recalls doing as a child fifty or so years ago? Others recall milk being ladled from the churn; and Mr Cyril Mather, who helped run the family Mayfield Dairy until his retirement in 1984, still possesses a pint and a half milk bottle of the type once delivered to customers. The memory of Pither's (Bell Street) famous warm pies and sausages still makes mouths water.

A look at old Henley newspapers makes enlightening reading, too. Advertisements are couched in a polite language which has long since gone: Alfred Haslam, 'Coal, Coke, Hay, Straw and Chaff, Friday Street . . . W.R. Norton, 15 customers for their patronage, and will endeavour always to merit it' (December 1881). Styles have changed: 'A genuine Eugene Wave, whole head 25s; Shingled head 21s: side pieces from 12s 6d. Up-to-date Saloon . . . W.R. Norton, 15 Reading Road' (December 1934). Social structures and requirements have changed: 'Wanted – Staid woman as Cook. Must be willing to make herself useful. Sober and respectable. Apply "Broad Gates", Henley'; 'Young Lady seeks employment as Governess or Lady's Companion. Musical' (August 1909).

The following photographs are of workaday Henley. A few of the occasions depicted are times when business could not go on as usual.

Hart Street was once known as High Street. This postcard, dating from around 1905, shows a rough-surfaced road with shallow gutters, but quite free of traffic congestion.

Clear improvements to the road, including deeper gutters, have been made by the time of this picture, probably taken in the early 1920s. Note the change in spelling of the Catherine Wheel Hotel. Records of a 'Catharine Wheel' inn at Henley go back to 1541 and probably refer to the inn on this site. The hotel was a part of Brakspear's, but was sold by the company in 1928 and now flourishes as a Berni Inn.

Above: The Catherine Wheel (right) has taken over the two private houses below it (seen with a ladder propped against them in the picture opposite). The view dates from the 1930s: the street lamps have been converted from gas to electric, road markings have appeared and there is a rather wooden policeman at the junction below the market place to help regulate the increasing traffic. Cars are already beginning to congest the street scene in the photograph below. Note, too, the sprouting bushes where today only traffic lights and bollards stand.

The old Town Hall. The town hall built in 1795 by William Bradshaw originally had an open ground floor or piazza which was used as a cornmarket. Around 1870, however, Henley Corporation enclosed this to provide themselves with more space indoors. This picture probably shows the building shortly after the work was carried out. In the background on the left (just above the head of the man by the cart) there is a sign jutting out which indicates the side entrance to Henley Fire Station.

The new Town Hall was built at the turn of the century, designed by the architect Henry T. Hare. As the stone flanked by workmen below records, it was constructed to commemorate the sixtieth year of the reign (1837–97) of Her Most Gracious Majesty Queen Victoria. (One wonders what the workman, top right of the picture, can be pointing at which is of more interest than the work in progress.) The completed Town Hall (above) once had iron gates at its entrance, but these were replaced by oak doors in 1909 – to keep out the draughts.

Tolls over Henley Bridge were abolished in 1873. The toll-house can be seen on the right.

Northfield End, *c.* 1917. The obelisk on the corner of Marlow Road (to the right of the picture) has been re-erected in Marsh Meadows by the river. It had stood in the town centre until 1885.

The Fair Mile, pre-1900, in the days when sheep grazed peacefully by the roadside, and elms (felled in 1953) graced the view. But if the absence of motor vehicles makes the road seem calm and safe, the *Henley Advertiser* of December 1881 contains a cautionary tale which shows there were other hazards to consider: 'ACCIDENT. On Wednesday afternoon, as Mrs Makins, of Rotherfield Court, was riding in the Fair Mile, the horse shied, and threw her somewhat heavily to the ground. She was conveyed home in a cab, and Mr Baines was soon in attendance, but happily no injury had been done. In less than half an hour, nothing daunted, Mrs Makins, to the surprise of many, was seen mounted on the same horse, riding through the town to continue her ride.'

Thames Side. In medieval times Henley flourished as a market town and river port. Grain, timber and stone were all conveyed along the Thames. But the arrival of trains in the nineteenth century hastened the decline of such river commerce, and by the time this picture was taken, in the late 1890s, river trade had already slumped. The building on the right, at the corner of Friday Street with Thames Side, was a granary and warehouse; in later years it was converted into the rather attractive riverside cottages that can be seen today.

Stocking the Thames. This turn of the century picture, taken from Thames Side, shows men stocking the Thames with fish, thought by Mr George Bushell, the owner of the photograph, to be trout. Miss Sybil Reeves supplies an anecdote from January 1902, found in her father's archives: 'A trout weighing 8lb leaped into a boat near Henley Bridge on a Regatta day a few years ago, and there have been other reports of the same thing happening at various spots near Henley on different occasions.' Mr Reeves was a very keen fisherman, although not particularly for trout.

Stanley Mead, 29 Duke Street. Stanley Mead's was a colourful business beyond compare. Advertisements in the *Henley Chronicle* of 1908 give an idea of the diversity of the activities he carried on in his Duke Street premises: 'Hairdresser, Tobacconist, Fishing Tackle Dealer and Thames Angler. Fish preserved and mounted. Old cases cleaned and repaired. First class work guaranteed. Umbrellas repaired and re-covered on the shortest notice.' Henley resident Mr John Crocker, who knew the Meads very well, has identified the figure crouching in the front of this particular picture as Stanley, and believes the lad to the right to be Sidney, the oldest of three Mead sons. Mr Crocker supplies further information: 'Stanley was very extrovert and in great demand at Smoking Concerts and Charity Concerts. I do not know the name of the wedding he is celebrating, but clearly he had

J. Hawkins, Duke Street. John Hawkins originally ran his grocery, glassware and china business in Bell Street, from the 1870s. In the 1880s, as he declared in the *Henley Advertiser*, it was 'The Best House in Henley for Glasses, Wicks, Lamps, etc etc.' Goods could be hired and lamps could be neatly mended. 'Oils! Oils! Oils! Bright burning oils, free from danger, smoke or smell.' Crystal oil, petroleum and paraffin all cost one shilling for a gallon, and 'finest benzine' cost one shilling and sixpence a gallon. The premises later moved to Duke Street, where Queen Mary was a visitor on more than one occasion – which certainly attracted the crowds, as this picture of around 1905 shows. The high-class glass, china and cutlery emporium continued in Duke Street until 1950.

(continued from previous page) hired a street organ and was acting the monkey. The cage with the Love Bird who picked out cards which purported to tell fortunes was a feature of street organs at that time. I would love to hear the recitations by the monkey now – no doubt unfit for my ears then!' The Stanley Mead business was in Duke Street for many years from the late Victorian period.

Bell Street, showing another example of the diversity of trade carried on under one name. The sign below the Half Way House announces 'W. Bunce, Fruiterer, Greengrocer, Potato Salesman.' Mr Bunce was the publican of the Half Way House during the 1870s and 1880s, but in common with many of the smaller innkeepers he carried on extra work to eke out a living. Another example of this practice was the publican of the Angel at Remenham who, in 1871, was also a journeyman bricklayer. He was assisted in the Angel by his wife and daughter (the latter was also a dressmaker). In addition, the publican took in two lodgers to help with family income.

Opposite page, top:
A works photograph of 1886, typical of the sort made for the customer or for sales purposes. It shows a beer wagon made for Greys Brewery by the Gloucester Wagon Works. Greys was a rival brewery to Brakspear's; it took its name from its situation on the south side of Friday Street in the parish of Rotherfield Greys. The business had been in existence since at least 1823, but its whole history was marked by a succession of different owners. By the mid-1880s it was owned by Frederick Holmes in conjunction with various partners who had brewing interests in Brighton and Stroud. Eventually, Brakspear's bought Greys Brewery in 1896. The Half Way House closed at this time.

Holton's Coal and Coke Factors, 1920s. Sidney Holton delivered coal which arrived by train at Henley (when there was a coalyard at the station). He was also mayor in 1928 and 1929. This picture in the Market Place shows a 'Guess the Correct Weight' competition in aid of the Mayor's Relief Fund. The prize is a lump of 'Conduit Shallow Kibble'.

The Old White Hart, Hart Street. This inn was mentioned in records as early as the 1480s. Some believe that its name derives from the fact that Richard II rode through the town just after the Peasants' Revolt in 1381 and so the inn took the White Hart, which was the King's badge, as its own emblem. Nowadays the courtyard where this Christmas market of 1927 is taking place – and where there used to be a weekly market for farmers – is a venue for eating and drinking. The farmer standing without a hat, third from the left on the far side of the left hand row of pig pens, has been identified as Mr Alfred Austin – who will appear again in the section on Hambleden. Francis Sheppard reports in his book, *Brakspear's Brewery*, that around 1800 the Old White Hart was one of the inns where illicit gambling with cards took place. On one occasion, in 1800, the town watchman reported hearing loud conversation in the Old White Hart in the early hours of the morning, and that he did not know how much was won or lost 'but that he heard the Money often sound on the Table'. Indeed, the landlord was known to have said to a prospective gambler, 'Man, we do not play for Crowns here, but for Guineas or a Bull's Eye,' – a hundred pound note, which was a small fortune.

J.S. Penicud, Dairyman is recorded as having premises at 16 Hart Street in 1928, previously Hughes Bros/Hughes Bros and Persey Dairyman 1908–1926. The people in this picture have been identified by Mr Cyril Mather, whose father Harold worked at the dairy around 1920, as: Mr Dick Jerome (van driver), Mr Ted May (pushing the milk cart), Mr Fred Girdler (in the doorway with Mr Penicud, who is wearing the trilby). Mr John Crocker provides the further information that the brick building to the left was an antique store, run by people named Goddard.

Mather and Sons. After working in Hart Street, Mr Harold Mather continued in his own dairy business: an eighth share in an Irish Sweepstake brought him enough money to buy a business and begin trading from Sheep House Farm, Reading Road in 1933. Pictured here are his sons, who joined the business. Left to right: George, Cyril and Ted. The business began with just a pony and cart, but by the 1940s and '50s it had three Ford vans.

Thirsty work. These individuals look as if they could sink more than a pint of milk! They are members of the workforce of John Moss, an agricultural machinist based at Northfield End. They are seen here in the 1850s in their workyard next to Leicester House. The beerhouse behind them, situated so conveniently for refreshment, is believed to be the Two Magpies. Mr Moss has been identified as the man wearing the top hat. The array of machinery shown includes (left) a tyring machine for wooden cartwheels, a potato seeder (middle), and a swede masher (right).

Opposite:
The family Mayfield Dairy enjoyed its fiftieth anniversary in 1983, by which time it was at Boston Road. Mr Cyril Mather is pictured here celebrating the occasion, delivering a pint to Mrs Hill of Wilson Avenue, who had received Mather milk for over fifty years. In 1984 the Mathers sold their business to Clifford's Dairies.

Red Lion Hotel. Perhaps the most renowned coaching inn in Henley is the Red Lion. Overlooking the river at the bottom of Hart Street, it was a favoured stopping off point for many an illustrious visitor. King Charles I stayed here in 1632 on his way to Oxford, and the Duke of Marlborough broke his journeys to Blenheim here, although he seems not to have left the comfort of his bed to chance, because he furnished his own room! It is even recorded that the Prince of Wales, later King George IV, ate fourteen mutton chops at a single sitting here. At least one landlord made his fortune at the Red Lion: a young man called Barrett March amassed £90,000 here in the eighteenth century, and retired to live at Bird Place, Remenham. This postcard shows the hotel some time before 1942, which is the date of the postmark.

The Busy Bee Foden steam wagon, *c*. 1900. In 1779 Robert Brakspear became a brewer in Henley and his descendants have dominated the local brewing trade ever since. The steam wagon was called *The Busy Bee* in an allusion to Brakspear's unofficial emblem of a bee. It was used for deliveries and is shown here leaving the Little Angel, Remenham, which is just out of view to the right.

Henley Volunteer Fire Brigade was set up in 1868. This rather contrived 'action shot', *c.* 1890, shows the men preparing their Merryweather 'Firefly' steam engine, the first non-manual engine the brigade had owned. They are obviously proud of it!

Ready for action. Seen here in 1900, the brigade is ready for fire fighting with its horse-drawn engine.

Horsepower of a different type moved this engine around. The brigade is seen here being presented with a new engine shortly after the Second World War.

And now to Henley children. Henley Grammar School, *c*. 1921. Mrs F. Povey (née Greenaway) supplied this picture and is the fourth girl from the left in the back row.

Sherwood House, Greys Road was a residential nursery for children from 1952 to 1982. The house has since been demolished and replaced by Sherwood Gardens retirement bungalows.

Children at Sherwood House, 1954. The children are seen here dressed smartly for the wedding of a former matron. Some of the children at Sherwood were orphans, but most were there because they needed care and protection. In the early years some babies stayed at the house while their mothers recovered from tuberculosis at a local sanatorium. The staff pictured are, left to right: Mrs Mackenzie, 'Peggs' Smith, Edna ?, Margaret Ayers, Dorothy Walman, Mavis ?.

Being taken for a ride, 1958. Miss Dorothy Walman lets the children push her around, while Mrs Witts looks on. Prams like this one are certainly not made today.

Sherwood House Gardens, 1959. This time the prams are being used in a more conventional manner. The staff are Miss Ivy Gray (left) and Miss Audrey Fisher (right).

Henley station. The first proposal for a railway line to Henley was made in 1833 but nothing came of it. The Great Western Railway gained permission in 1847 to set up a link between the town and the main line at Twyford, but again, nothing was actually done. It was not until 1857, and with a good deal of encouragement from the local population, that the GWR opened the Henley–Twyford route. One of the busiest times for the station is, of course, Regatta week, when business is far from usual. This picture from 1952 shows the station decorated in preparation for its influx of visitors. It is doubtful that in that year they had quite the staffing shortage of 1901/2, however, when, to meet the demand of extra trains and passengers flocking to Henley, men from as far afield as Hereford, Chester and even Liskeard had to be brought in to help. Over the years, more people have had cars to transport them and there has been less pressure on trains.

Floods. Not for nothing does the Thames derive its name from a Celtic word meaning 'dark water'. Over the years flooding has been a considerable problem, until the Thames Conservancy and Thames Water Authority improved the systems of water flow control. Particularly bad floods have been recorded for the years 1774, 1809 and 1894. And with the floods has come disruption to Henley's day-to-day life, as the following pages show. The above picture of the Two Brewers, Remenham was taken during the flood of 1894.

To paddle or not to paddle, that seems to be the question being weighed by the boys on the right. It is thought they are in Remenham Lane, but the exact date is not known.

The Two Brewers was flooded again in the 1940s.

The old wooden bridge at Henley, it is said, was swept away by the flood waters of 1774. The present bridge has stood the test of time since 1786. On the right of this picture can be seen the Carpenter's Arms, which was replaced by the Royal Regatta headquarters in 1986.

Camping punts for hire – but you would need a punt to reach them! This picture was taken, probably in the 1940s, at the bottom of New Street and Wharfe Lane, and shows the Regatta stretch.

The Angel Hotel, now called The Angel (on the Bridge), *c.* 1940s.

'The remarkable snow storm.' That is how the *Henley Chronicle* described the snowfall of April 1908, when it was reported that at least a foot of snow settled, disrupting the life of the town. 'Business was at a deadlock. People would not leave their fireside unless absolutely compelled. Many shops closed long before the usual hour on Saturday evening. It would have been a waste of gas to keep open.' Many trees and houses were damaged, and there was the danger of avalanches of snow sliding from the roofs so that 'people . . . had to walk charily along the road lest they should be buried beneath the falling snow'.

SECTION THREE

Recreation, Celebration and Demonstration

Before every household acquired a television set, recreation was a great deal more active, involving whole days spent blackberrying or mushrooming, or simply walking; games played by children, like skipping, tip-cat and hopskotch, did not require any of the sophisticated equipment which seems to be essential for so many of today's games. Youngsters joined the Scouts and the Boys Brigade and men joined the Town Band – in numbers it would be hard to equal today. There were also regular visits to the Kenton Theatre, which still provides entertainment, and to the Palace Cinema, now closed. The selection of pictures on the next few pages recalls some of the personal pleasures and public celebrations enjoyed by Henley residents over the years.

Walking on water. The adverse weather conditions which could totally disrupt business life also provided local people with new possibilities for recreation! During the hard winter of 1895, when the above picture was taken, the Thames froze for several weeks. Not only could people skate on the ice, but carriages were driven over it. The view here is downstream of the Henley Bridge, approximately opposite Phyllis Court.

Calmer waters. This tranquil scene with a fisherman, of around 1887, shows the Regatta course, looking towards Temple Island in the distance. Jerome K. Jerome, in *Three Men in a Boat*, written at this time, proclaims, 'I never knew anybody catch anything up the Thames, except minnows and dead cats. . . .' In fact, fishing over some stretches, such as between Hampton Court and Pangbourne, would have been quite good. Certain areas were renowned for particular fish: the river at Henley was considered good for roach; fly fishing was best pursued just below Hambleden Weir; Windsor was the place for trout.

Rambling jaunts have always been popular, and this howitzer, which used to be on a site near the bowling green along Mill Meadows, was once a favourite resting place. There were two howitzers, relics from the First World War, but it is thought they were removed for use as scrap metal during the Second World War. This picture shows (on the right) Miss Gladys Neal (to reappear in the Shiplake section) and a friend in the 1920s.

The bathing pool along the Wargrave Road, where the Henley Rowing Club is now. Mrs Avril Bryant, who supplied the postcard, remembers learning to swim there as a child on outings with Nettlebed Primary School in the early 1950s. The bathing pool closed in the 1980s.

'Girls, also, don't look half bad in a boat, if prettily dressed,' said Jerome K. Jerome. And the *Thames Times and Fashionable Gazette* remarked of a certain type of woman who enjoyed boating purely for its aesthetic side: 'You will never see an oar in her white hands. Indeed there is often nothing visible belonging to her but a big Japanese parasol.' In the 1920s, when this picture was taken, the Japanese parasol was still *de rigueur*.

Charabanc outing from Henley, 1920s. Another popular – and sedate – treat: note the speed restriction of 12 m.p.h. written on the bottom of the vehicle at the back. The group is seen passing along Hart Street.

'Watermans and Fishermans, 1923' is the handwritten message on the back of this old photograph. The crowds are clearly outside the Red Lion Hotel, being kept back from the river by a policeman. Could it be the occasion of river races between watermen and fishermen? Nobody has been able to confirm this.

Celebrating the coronation of King Edward VII and Queen Alexandra, 1902. There is no doubt about this occasion. The location is Bell Street and shows Machin's butchers shop and Crocker's shoe shop (where Waitrose's wine department now stands). The people in the picture have been identified by Mr John Crocker, now 88 years old, as his grandfather, Mr Henry Crocker (second right, in the shoe shop doorway), with Mrs Crocker and a daughter Mabel (in the windows above). On the left are Mr and Mrs Edward Machin. Mrs Machin, christian name Emily, was the eldest daughter of Mr Henry Crocker. Mr John Crocker relates that his father and grandfather painted the portrait of King Edward, which fits the space between the shop windows, from a magazine picture. The shop was a prizewinner in the shop-dressing competition held as part of the coronation celebrations. Mr Crocker adds: 'With a powerful glass, one can read the label on some ladies' Balmoral boots in the window – 3/11,' and, further, 'Butchers and fishmongers shops did not have glass windows in those days; they were all open to the road which was gravel and watered in the summer.'

A tea party, held on the Market Place. The occasion was the coronation of King George V and Queen Mary in 1911.

Silver Jubilee decorations in Bell Street, 1935, to celebrate the twenty-fifth year of the reign of King George V.

The Fire Brigade parade through Henley. It is thought that this picture shows the brigade on the way to the official opening on 5 June 1923 of the War Memorial Hospital in Harpsden Road.

The suffragettes commanded quite an audience in front of the Town Hall in 1909 when they spoke up for the rights of women.

Maypole dancing in the 1920s provides a calmer scene. Again, the venue is in front of the Town Hall. How many different crowds and moods has it borne silent witness to over the years?

Empire Day march, Hart Street. Empire Day was first instituted in 1902 after the end of the Boer War. Its initiator was the Earl of Meath and its purpose was to encourage schoolchildren to be aware of their duties and responsibilities as citizens of the British Empire. In 1958 it was renamed Commonwealth Day. The date suggested for this picture is 1909, possibly 1911. One hopes that the apparent dampness of the day did not affect the children's enthusiasm!

Fancy dress ball at Henley Town Hall, 1900s. The man just right of centre in the front row looks as if he is dressed as one of the pierrots who provided musical entertainment at the Regatta.

Dare one say: more fancy dress? The mayor and aldermen are seen here ‘at work’ in the 1890s in rather studied poses.

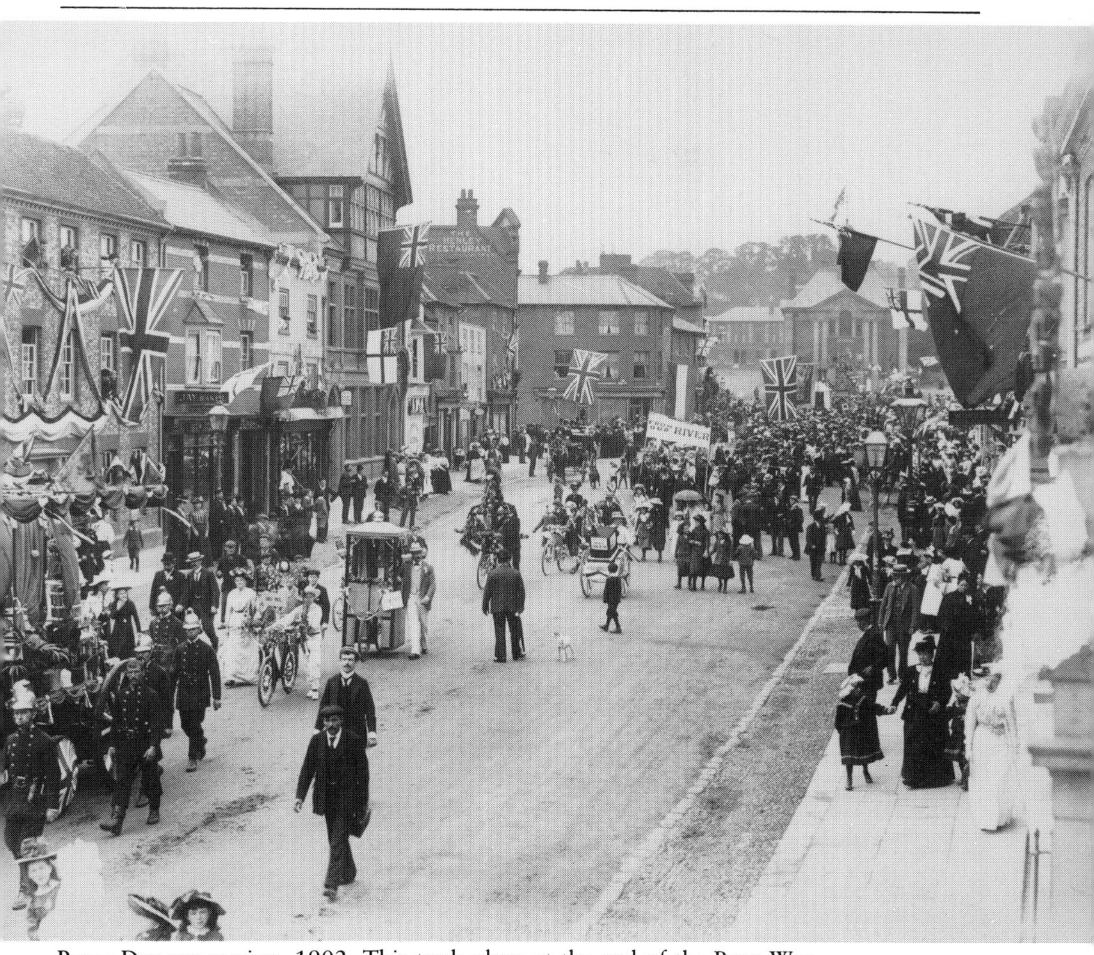

Peace Day procession, 1902. This took place at the end of the Boer War.

Henley pram race, 1964. Those versatile prams (two on the right) from Sherwood House line up for the off: 'Modern Mothers' are (top) Miss Pat Noble and Miss Vivienne Gardner (bottom); those representing 'The Plague' have not been identified!

'H. Mather & Sons', a milk pram pushed by Cyril Mather on Carnival Day 1963 to celebrate thirty years of the family's milk delivery business. The old-fashioned pram might well have been more reliable than modern motorized transport on one near-disastrous Easter Sunday around 1950. At that time the Mathers received their milk from the Milk Marketing Board at Newbury. At 2 a.m. they rose as usual to bottle the milk which was delivered to them in ten 10 gallon churns. But, to their horror, it was all sour. So Cyril and his father Harold jumped into their van to drive to Newbury for fresh milk – only to break down half way. Luckily though, brother George was following in a back-up van and the first van was abandoned by the road. After their mad dash they found the police awaiting them back at the dairy, wanting an explanation of the circumstances in which the vehicle had been left. One wonders if the customers ever knew how much effort went into the delivery of their milk that morning?

Opposite:
'That Was The Winter That Was' – a play on the title of the sixties television programme as well as a reference to the hard winter of 1962/3 – won first prize in the carnival of 1963. Driving the float is Mr Ted Mather.

Scouts. The Henley-on-Thames (YMCA) Scout Group, formed in 1908, was one of the first troops to be set up in the country. This picture was taken in the first years of their formation. The *Henley Standard* of August 1909 contains an interesting report on one of their early activities, an annual camp on the Isle of Wight. Despite inclement weather, the scouts undertook marches and outings, such as an evening sea trip to Bournemouth where 'the troop had rather more than an hour on shore'. The report continues, 'A very keen interest has been displayed in the Orderly and Tent Kit Inspection Competitions,' and 'Discipline has been well maintained throughout, and the whole Troop has benefitted in every way by the ten days spent under canvas.'

Henley Boys Brigade march to their camp in 1909, past the Catherine Wheel in Hart Street. One hopes discipline was as well maintained as at the scout camp.

Football on Good Friday. The dashing footballers seen here made up the GWR and GPO teams for a soccer match played on Good Friday 1901 at the corner of Marlow Road.

Henley YMCA FC during the 1923/4 season.

Another team effort – but what was the reason for the Town Band taking to the water? The date on the back of the photograph is the only clue: 1922/3. Whatever the occasion, the men look rather muffled up against the weather.

Henley Town Band looking happier on terra firma, this time *c.* 1925 in front of the Town Hall.

SECTION FOUR

Around Hambleden

'I would like to keep quiet about Hambleden, to lock it away in its valley and let no one know of it. . . . The village of Hambleden is the American's dream of England.' These words were written by Cecil Roberts in *Gone Afield* (1936), and similar sentiments could be expressed today. Hambleden retains the charm and tranquillity of the typical village. It is fortunate, too, in that it still enjoys amenities which other villages of its size and proximity to larger centres of population have lost: a village shop and post office, and a doctor's surgery. But its butchers has closed, and there is no longer a school, bakers or blacksmiths as there were in earlier years.

Although small, Hambleden has always been a place of some note. There was a Roman settlement there, with a large colony at Mill End, and many coins and valuables dating from this period have been found. They were once deposited in Hambleden's own museum, but since this has been replaced by the estate office, they have been moved to museums elsewhere. In Norman times Hambleden was liable to a tax of 20 hides, compared with Marlow's 15 hides, and Fingest's and Fawley's 10 hides apiece. So it must have been a manor of some significance in the district. It also has a claim to fame as the birthplace of Saint Thomas de Cantilupe (1218–82), the last pre-Reformation saint, who was canonized in 1320.

On a more modern and secular note, Hambleden can take some credit for the creation of the Henley Regatta. The first rowing race between Oxford and Cambridge University crews took place in 1829 over the stretch of the Thames from Hambleden Lock to Henley Bridge. It was the excitement that this and subsequent races involving the two universities generated which led the townspeople of Henley to think an annual regatta of their own would make an entertaining and commercial proposition.

Over the following pages we make a trip back in time to Hambleden, 'a village in a valley' as its name suggests, and to some of the fine houses in the area, finishing at the beautiful river-side Medmenham.

Hambleden Lock, *c*. 1875. 'Sweet Hambleden lock,' as Jerome K. Jerome called it, looks the picture of peace and tranquillity in the days when it was hand operated. The lock-keeper at Hambleden from 1777 to 1836 was Caleb Gould, a most interesting character reputed to eat a plate of onion porridge every night. It must have done him good because he lived to the ripe old age of 92.

St Mary the Virgin, *c.* 1900. The font of Hambleden's church is thought to date from the twelfth century or possibly even earlier, being the survivor of a Saxon church built here around 670–1000. The original Norman church was built here 1100–1200, but there have been numerous later additions, such as the western tower (1719–21), and much rebuilding. St Thomas de Cantilupe was baptized in the church. A curious tale surrounds two of the bells at Hambleden, the treble and smaller Sanctus. They are thought to have been cast from the two bells of Fingest church lost by the rector of Fingest at a game of cards with the rector of Hambleden. The Sanctus bell, dated 1730, vanished from the church around 1796, but turned up again in 1954, by which time a successor had already been ordered. So it now makes an unusual lampshade in the belfry! One of the people to record the tale of the gambling of Fingest's bells (which has variations) was Wilfred Watts, a former rector of Hambleden. When he first became rector, in 1937, he earned himself the name of the 'Red Rector' because he removed all the cards which reserved the best pews for the local gentry, and took away the notice at the back of the church which reserved pews for the poor of the parish. He only left the cards reserving pews for the patron of the living (Lord Hambleden) and the churchwardens. Although somewhat taken aback, most people soon accepted the 'revolution'. A visit to St Mary's today shows the church much as it appears in the above picture, although the railings on the right in front of the churchyard wall have been removed.

A wedding party outside the village hall, Hambleden, when wedding dress fashion was calf-length. The happy couple were Hambleden residents 'Arthur' and 'Eddey', uncle and aunt of Mr Alf Austin, from whose album all the following family pictures have come. Second from the right is Mr Sid Baker who ran Stag's Stores, an off-licence and general store at Pheasants Hill. It is recalled with smiles that if closing time passed and men were still thirsty for beer he simply pulled a discreet curtain and let them continue!

The Stag and Huntsman is still to be found in Hambleden, little changed from this view, but what was being celebrated on the occasion of this picture (*c.* 1920s) is lost in time.

Eliza and John Dawson, who lived at Hambleden, seen in the early 1900s. Eliza was grandmother of Mr Alf Austin. For a while she lived as caretaker in the Hambleden museum, now the estate office. She had ten children (one being Eddey, seen on her wedding day on the opposite page) and lived to be 103. Even in her eighties this remarkable lady would walk along the towpath to the Regatta at Henley.

Mr Alfred Austin, father of Alf, who had a milk, poultry and eggs round. The picture shows his first van, acquired in 1932, when he moved to Pheasants Hill Farm. Mr Austin senior was the farmer identified at the Old White Hart on p. 38.

Pheasants Hill Farm, where Mr Austin senior was tenant farmer until 1961. It is now a private house, although the farm buildings, including the granary, remain. Seen here in the 1940s are Mr Victor Bird (left) and Arthur ? holding open the gate.

Mr Bird ploughs his furrow, 1930s. The scene presents an idyllic picture to an era used to mechanized farming, but behind the idyll was a lot of hard manual work.

Loading swedes. Mr George Ansell senior, an employee of the farm, at work during the Second World War.

Fawley Court, between Henley and Hambleden, seen in the 1880s from the opposite tow-path. The mixed fortunes of Fawley, which dates in parts to the twelfth century, include damage by Royalists during the Civil War as well as redesign by Wren and, later, James Wyatt. During the Second World War it was requisitioned by the Army and left in a state of neglect, but, fortunately, the house was restored by the Polish Congregation of Marian Fathers, who bought it in 1952. The retreat centre and pilgrims house there are open all year round, and the museum is open from March to November.

Parmoor, pre-1907. The father of Sir Stafford Cripps once lived at Parmoor, and King Zog of Albania lived there during the Second World War. In 1947 St Katharine's Convent made it their home.

Greenlands, *c.* 1882. Jerome K. Jerome called Greenlands 'the rather uninteresting-looking river residence of my newsagent', a reference to its ownership by W.H. Smith, who became Viscount Hambleden. Yet the history of Greenlands is far from uninteresting. Like Fawley Court, it was caught up in the havoc of the Civil War, but fortunately it too has flourished this century. Taken over from Lord Hambleden, it now enjoys a reputation as one of the foremost training centres for business management, the Henley Management College, which was incorporated in 1945 and granted a royal charter in 1991.

The Thames from the Abbey lawn, Medmenham, *c.* 1883. A record of halcyon days by the river. The two men in the foreground are quite happy to pose a while for the camera but the third, in the background, seems anxious to be off rowing.

Danesfield House, Medmenham, *c.* 1875. The genteel scene of tea on the lawn is at a far remove from the area's turbulent history, when the Danes pillaged their way along the Thames from the eighth to tenth centuries. They had a camp at Danesfield, or Danes' Field. The house today is a hotel.

A ferry journey, *c.* 1890, with the Ferry Hotel on the left and the Abbey on the right. There was an interesting dispute involving the ferry and the landlord of the Ferry Hotel in 1899. The landlord was operating the ferry to his own profit, yet many believed it was a public one. The argument ended up in the Court of Appeal, which decided that the ferry was indeed public. A monument, which can still be seen, was erected to commemorate the victory, although the ferry no longer operates. Medmenham Abbey is famous – or notorious – for the so-called Hell Fire Club, founded by Sir Francis Dashwood of West Wycombe in 1745. The club was renowned for indulging in all sorts of black magic and orgies when it met there, a far cry from the peaceful behaviour of the Cistercian order which lived at the abbey in the thirteenth century, or from the tranquil scene it offers today.

Medmenham church: the exterior from the south, *c.* 1880. The view has hardly changed today, although the churchyard looks tidier.

Medmenham village, *c.* 1890, with the church in the background. This picture is taken in Ferry Lane. The house on the left is the same today, although the frontage is better maintained, but the view up towards the hill is now obscured by a house which bears a date stone of 1896, and by trees which have grown up over the last century.

SECTION FIVE

Around Shiplake

Vicar of this pleasant spot
Where it was my chance to marry,
Happy, happy be your lot –
You were he that knit the knot!

Thus Tennyson recorded his delight when he was married at Shiplake's church in 1850. And, indeed, Shiplake is a pleasant spot. Divided between the old village and the river-side Lower Shiplake, it is attractive and quiet.

But that is not to say there have not been some quite striking changes in recent years. New estates have been built in Lower Shiplake, and where a modest station complete with welcoming buildings once stood, there is now little more than a plain platform. A coal fire once burned in the cosy waiting room and porters happily carried passengers' luggage right to their doorsteps. Once a week an army of fishermen would come down by train from London and disembark here, ready for a day's fishing along the river. Such scenes are no more, but at least the station is still used (tickets are sold on the train itself), which is more than can be said for many more rural halts in other parts of the country.

This section records some of the changes which have taken place in and around the village, and across the river in Wargrave. It also includes pictures from the time of the Second World War (during my research I came across very few photographs from this period): of the Red Cross convalescent home for men of the Armed Forces at Harpsden, where Gillott's School is now, and of one of the most familiar faces in the area at that time, the district nurse. She is one of the people singled out for special mention in Thomas B. Scotcher's charming account of life on the home front at Binfield Heath, *An English Village in Wartime*. For those interested in that period, Scotcher provides some colourful minutiae of village life and some carefully recorded statistics. For example: the village raised £300 in addition to the money supplied by the Government for knitting wool; the total weight of wool knitted was 16 cwt and the total number of garments knitted for servicemen by the village knitting circle 4,275! He even lists these by type, from 647 pairs of socks to 3 chest protectors and just 2 pairs of bedsocks (one wonders how the lucky recipients of the latter were chosen).

Mill Road, Shiplake Village. This view hardly altered until after the Second World War, when a housing estate was built on the field to the left. The tall elms have gone and another estate, including homes for the elderly, has appeared in the field behind. The cottages on the right are, however, still there.

Station Road, opposite Mill Road, Lower Shiplake. The curious feature of this picture (probably 1950s) is that it shows the telephone box on the corner beside the village shop. These days it has been transplanted across the road to the near corner. One wonders why. Otherwise this scene remains much the same.

Shiplake railway station. Although this picture was taken as recently as 1963, the scene today has completely changed. The grand footbridge over the railway and the station buildings have gone, to be replaced by a small hut. The station is still used, but does not compare with that recalled by Miss Mary Burge, who supplied this view: 'The waiting room welcomed travellers with a coal fire and there were always porters on hand to help with luggage. They would even push trollies and trunks through the streets to the passenger's doorstep!'

First steps along Mill Road in the early years of this century. The little girl pictured with her sisters is Gladys Neal, the young lady seen sitting on the howitzer along the river from Henley on p. 58. Gladys later worked as a children's nanny in Shiplake, Henley, Wargrave, Sonning and London.

Gladys Neal with her brothers and sisters in 1908. Gladys and her twin brother (who died six months later) are the babes in arms. Despite the poor quality of the snapshot, it gives a good record of the clothes children used to wear.

The Plough Hotel, now the Plowden Arms, on the junction of the road to Binfield Heath with the Reading–Henley road. In her *History of Shiplake*, Emily Climenson records that the Plough was always the venue for a dinner after parish meetings and that this practice continued as late as 1870. From 1868 to around 1942, the Plough/Plowden Arms was tenanted by several generations of the Porter family. For at least some of that time they combined keeping the inn with trading as carpenters and undertakers. The exact date of this picture is not known, but it is probably around the turn of the century, and it could possibly show members of the Porter family, but nobody has been able to confirm this.

Thames at Shiplake. To take this picture today, showing Henley Sailing Club in the background, a photographer would have to sneak down a private road. But he would be unlikely to find the boats moored at the near bank since the boatyard (hidden by the car) is now also private property.

Dabchick houseboat. This postcard is a reminder of the turn-of-the-century heyday of the houseboat. The *Dabchick* was moored at Shiplake.

Camping at the Lock Meadow, Shiplake, *c.* 1895. Camping was a popular pursuit at this time, as readers of Charles Dickens junior's *Dictionary of the Thames*, published in 1888, will know. His comments on the matter, however, suggest he was not a great enthusiast: 'Camping out is a form of entertainment which has lately come into fashion, and is spoken of with much enthusiasm by its devotees, among whom may be numbered a proportion of ladies.' Yet, he continues, 'It is a little difficult to see the great enjoyment of sleeping in a tent when you can get a bed, or of being exposed to the mists and fogs which are so plentiful on the river at night and in the early morning even in the summer.'

Shiplake Lock around the turn of the century (above) and (below) around the 1920s. The view below can be compared with that on p. 96, when the old mill was still standing.

View above Shiplake Lock, *c.* 1880. It is difficult to decide whether these rowers are enjoying their outing or not!

The mill at Shiplake. The picture below, showing the low white footbridge, is taken from a similar vantage point as that on p. 94. The paper mill was demolished at the turn of the century – only the name of Mill Road suggests to the modern visitor that it ever existed. These pictures date from the late 1800s.

View from the ferry, Wargrave, *c.* 1887. A ferry between Wargrave and Shiplake existed from very early times, according to the Missenden Charters, and foot passengers were charged one halfpenny each.

The High Street, Wargrave, 1903. Note the hitching posts outside the White Hart on the left. This street remains remarkably similar today, although the Manor Cottages on the right have had wooden window shutters added and the large tree at the bottom corner of the street has gone – and, of course, the road has been improved.

Another view of the High Street, this time from the opposite end. On the left is the old Wargrave Coffee Tavern and Barbers Shop, while the White Hart can be seen in the distance on the right.

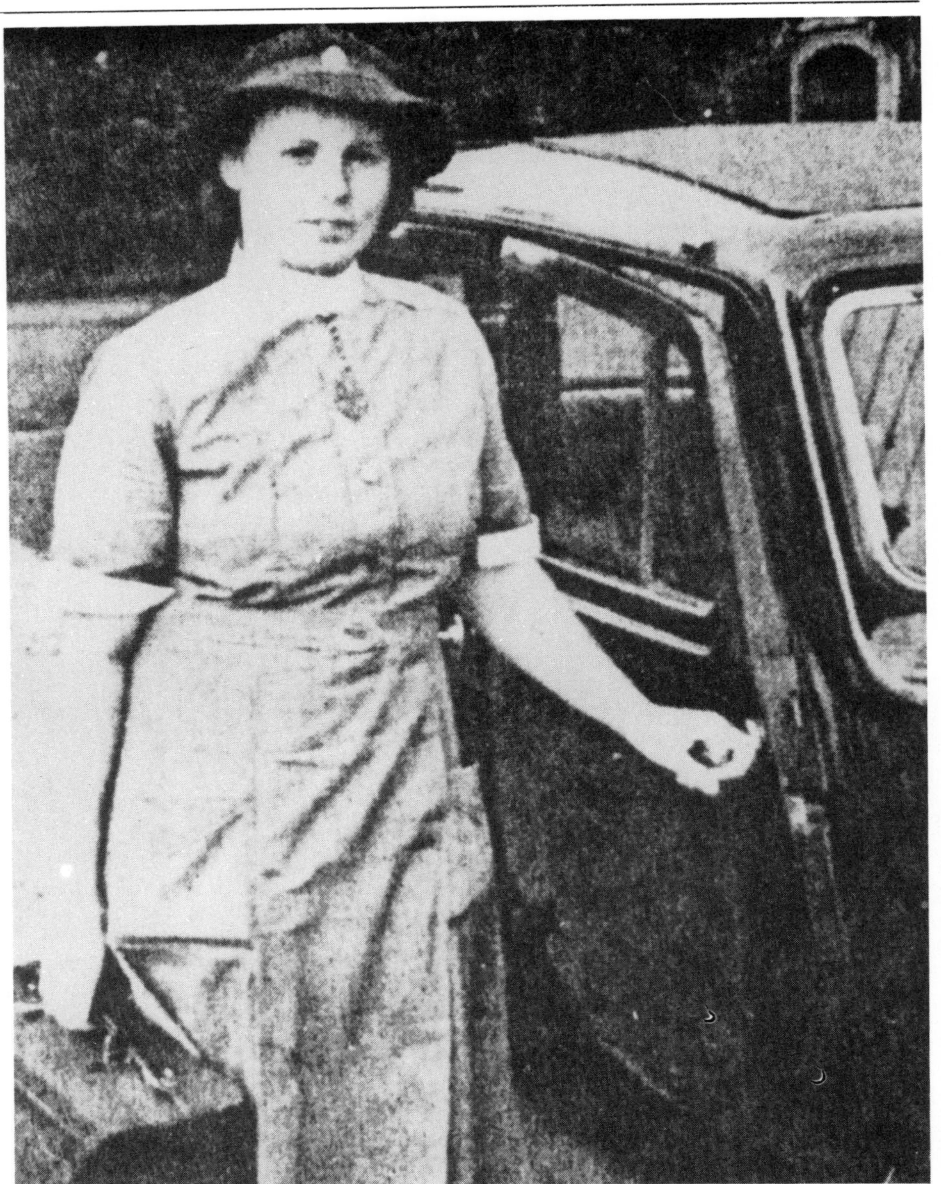

District Nurse Waterman during the Second World War. This picture takes us back across the river to Binfield Heath. Nurse Waterman is described in Thomas B. Scotcher's *An English Village in Wartime* (1945) as one of the 'important people' of Binfield Heath: 'She seems to know all the map spottings of the stork targets in Shiplake, Binfield Heath and adjoining Harpsden, Dunsden and Peppard.' He numbers her missions of mercy to the old and sick as 2,500 annually.

A corner of the village of Dunsden, 1949. Perhaps Nurse Waterman frequented this quiet road.

Gillott's, Harpsden, 1940s. Now converted into a school and looking quite different, Gillott's was used during the Second World War as a Red Cross convalescent home for men of the Armed Forces.

The staff at Gillott's. On the left, with glasses, is Mrs Reeves, the assistant quartermaster, and next to her in the back row is Mrs Barlow. Back row, second right is Betty Hiscock. Mrs Mary Adams, who was the cook at Gillott's and who supplied these pictures, recalls life at the home as a happy one: the men generally kept cheerful, even though they might be ill, and they helped with chores such as washing up after meals. They appreciated beyond measure the care from the nurses and staff, as many a verse presented to Mrs Adams (née Morgan) shows. One, 'A Soldier's Dream', conveys the thanks of a soldier who has come to Gillott's:

Then you find it strange among kindly nurses
To be away from your sergeant's curses,
And although fatigues must be done,
We like to do them just for fun . . .
At mealtimes there is something new
To get your food without a queue.
The fare is far beyond description
With no fear of indigestion:
No better food you'll buy in town
As cooked by Morgan and Nurse Brown . . .
In my opinion folks like these
Will bring old Hitler to his knees.

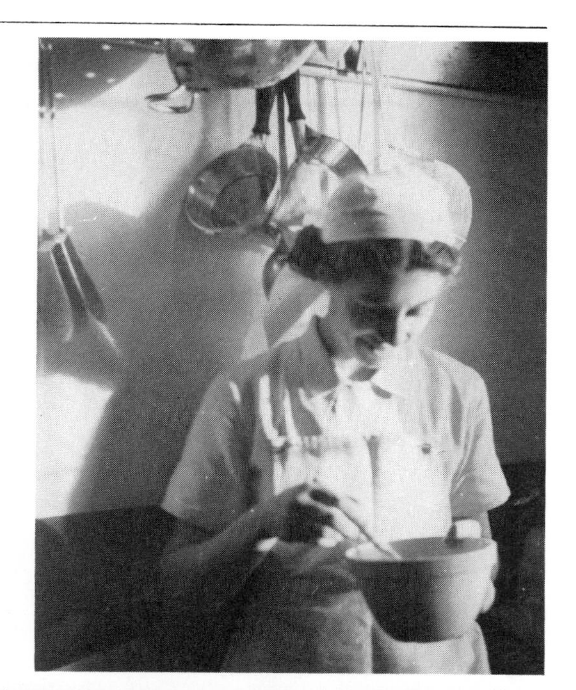

What's cooking? Miss Mary Morgan (later Adams) recalls that improvisation and inspiration were the order of the day in times of shortage. Yet the results were always palatable. The picture shows Miss Morgan in the kitchen at Gillott's.

Time to relax. Right: Hope Daniel and Alice Reynolds, with Dinah Deverill in front. Left: Rosemary Harding, Mary Morgan (in white), with Gloria Hudson in front. The name of the cloaked nurse is unknown.

Showtime. The men used to put on shows and entertainments to amuse themselves and the staff. Here, one swaps his uniform for less conventional attire.

In the early days at Gillott's patients wore their service uniforms. Later, they were issued with 'Hospital Blues': blue serge suits, white shirts and red ties.

SECTION SIX

Around Stoke Row

In the past Stoke Row and Highmoor were desperately impoverished communities. Isolated, served only by poor tracks until quite recent times, and lacking in water supply, they bred tough people. Indeed, the Chilterns as a whole were, from early times, notorious for being infested by lawless bands: in Henry II's day stewards had to be appointed to enforce forest law and maintain order in the district. The inaccessibility of the Chilterns made it a good place to which vagabonds might escape.

Today the area presents a completely different picture. Some older cottages have been swept away and others modernized. The mellowing council houses of the 1920s and '40s, coupled with the more spasmodic private building of later years, suggest a lively community in an enviable rural setting.

The surrounding woods are beautiful. Woodland crafts used to be a major industry of the area: chairleg-turning or bodging, tent peg making, the fashioning of farm implements, and so on. Bodging was carried on until as late as 1958 by Silas Saunders but tent pegging declined after the Second World War. Laureen Williamson, in her authoritative article 'The Lost Tent-peggers who made Millions' (*The Countryman*, 1985) explains that the craft, practised locally since at least the late 1800s, lost many of the men returning from the war to more lucrative employment at, for example, the (now closed) Star Brush factory. Yet at the beginning of the Second World War there were an estimated 100 peggers working around Stoke Row, and they produced some 30 million wooden tent pegs for the war effort. The hand-cleft peg is no longer made here, although it is in some parts of the country, such as the Cotswolds.

This section begins with these woodland crafts and the people associated with them. We meet other people, too. In small, enclosed communities such as this family memories are good and many names have been recalled – quite a feat when it comes to identifying members of the Stoke Row and Checkendon Home Guard on p. 115. From people, we move on to buildings, some now vanished, and to the activities at Highmoor School which have since been ended as a result of its closure in the 1960s. Finally, we go further afield, to the woods again, and then on a brief outing through the neighbouring area.

Tent pegs drying near Stoke Row, 1934. The life of the tent peg maker (pegger) was a hard one. He would often rise early in the morning and have a journey on foot or bicycle of several miles to reach his makeshift cabin in the woods, where he would spend twelve hours at his work. It is estimated that one man could make around 600–700 standard 12 inch pegs in a day. In 1885 he could expect to be paid 10d per 100; in the 1930s the rate was 1s 6d and in the 1940s, 1s 10d. The lengthening stack of pegs piled drying outside his cabin gives an indication of the success of his day.

Opposite:
Bunny Webb shaves a billet for tent pegs in the woods near Stoke Row, 1934. Laureen Williamson describes the techniques of the pegger and bodger thus: 'After a tree was felled the pegger would cross-cut the trunk to lengths to suit the pegs he was making (4 inches to 36 inches) and the bodger would cross-cut to the standard chair length. Next, these log lengths were split into billets (quartered) with slightly different tools, the pegger using a molly and flammer, the bodger a beetle and wedge. After this, their work diverged, the pegger sawing a rope notch in his billet before shaving the peg to final

shape, the bodger shaving his billet to a rough leg before finely turning it on a lathe. Both men sat astride identical 'horses', which clamped the billets while they shaved them with a two-handled drawshave.' Mr Bunny Webb, like the majority of woodcraft workers, was self-employed. During the Second World War he was one of several men who worked in sheds at the Cherry Tree pub, whose licencee (Mr Edwin Stallwood) was also a timber merchant. In 1942, Mr Stallwood was commissioned to supply one million tent pegs for the Armed Forces.

James Cox, master carpenter, builder and undertaker, with his wife and three of his children, *c.* 1890. Mr James Cox came from a long line of carpenter-joiners from the parish of Shiplake. In 1852 he married Eliza, the daughter of his employer, carpenter Mr James Giles, and they raised fourteen children in the Giles's house at Stoke Row, shown here. Their twelfth child, Albert, carried on the carpentry business until his death in 1967. The history of ownership of the house is one of remarkable continuity, although its name has undergone some interesting changes over the years. Built in *c.* 1650–75, it was occupied from at least the early 1700s by the Giles family and their heirs until 1967. In 1861 the property was known as Nos 1 and 2 Giles Cottages, whereas the census of 1871 recorded it as Carpenter's House – for obvious reasons; at the time of the 1891 census it was West End, possibly because the enumerator was thinking of the west end of the village; some time after the turn of the century it was known as The Rest, a reflection, possibly, of the undertaking business its inhabitants carried on; in 1975 it was renamed Bodgers, an echo of the craft widely practised in Stoke Row in former times.

Hide and seek. This picture shows the side of the Giles/Cox family's house, *c.* 1880, with the joiner's shed to the right and carefully posed figures half hidden in the garden.

'Young Mr Cox' (Thomas, son of James) stands hand on hip in front of the family home, with employees of the Cox carpentry business, *c.* 1890. In the middle at the back of the picture is the coffin shop (now gone, although brass plates have been found in the garden).

Harry Arthur Cox (left) and Albert William Cox (right), the thirteenth and twelfth children of James and Eliza Cox. The estimated date of this picture is around 1880. Note the practice of dressing little boys in dresses.

Harry Arthur Cox became a builder and worked from Foundry Cottage in Checkendon.

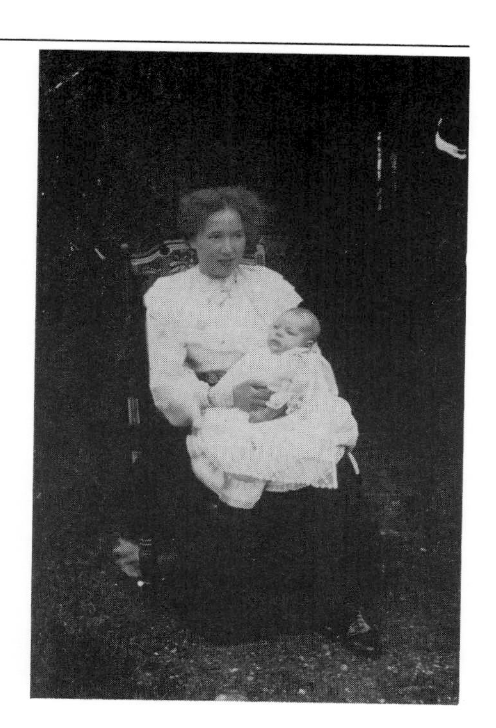

Mrs Louisa Cox, wife of Harry Arthur, and their daughter Winifred, aged six months, in 1908.

Winifred Cox, aged three years, carefully posed for what must have been a studio picture, 1911: a delightful reminder of the fashions of the time.

Sarah Tracey Saunders. Sarah was the landlady of the Crooked Billet at Stoke Row from the late nineteenth century until 1936. The picture is hard to date exactly because of its formal setting and the studied pose of the subject, but it could be as late as the Edwardian era.

The Crooked Billet public house. The young lad holding the dog is Ernie Fowles, with Mrs Fowles behind him. Next to them, in the back row are: Charlie Saunders (who died in 1935 when the cess-pit he was cleaning at the Black Horse, Checkendon exploded) and his brother Percy, Tracey, the spinster daughter of Mrs Sarah Tracey Saunders (she helped her mother to run the pub during the First World War) and Sarah Tracey herself, with Mr George ? on the end. It is thought that the two girls in the front are Beatty and 'young Tracey'. The suggested date for the picture is around 1930.

The Cherry Tree, Stoke Row. The Cherry Tree was first known as the Traveller's Friend and was almost certainly not licensed until the Beer Act of 1830. Its later name derives from the fact that Stoke Row was famous for its cherries and the inn was the rendezvous for coachloads of cherry pickers, some of whom bed-and-breakfasted there. The pickers collected from many private gardens and orchards, and also from the Maharajah's Well orchard which had been ceremonially planted with 101 cherry trees in 1864. This picture pre-dates 1858, as an extension built in that year is not yet in place.

A charabanc trip from outside the Cherry Tree, *c.* 1919. The Stallwood family – father Edwin, son Percy and grandson Ken (the present landlord) – have run the pub for over seventy years. The following people have been identified in the picture. Ladies, left to right: Miss Asa Lester, Mrs Harriet Stallwood with baby, Doris Stallwood, Maggie Stallwood, Mrs Emily Carter, Miss Jessie Stallwood, Mrs Florence Stallwood. Of the men, only Mr David Stallwood (fourth right in front of the charabanc) and Percy Stallwood (lad seated middle front) could be identified.

Stoke Row and Checkendon Home Guard: a more sombre gathering of the inhabitants of a later era. The following men have been identified. Back row: 4th from the left Mr Percy Collis, 5th Mr Stan Norris, 6th Mr 'Tavey' Franklin, 10th Mr George Lee. Middle row: 2nd from the left Mr Wally Slade, 3rd Mr Reg Denslow, 4th Mr William Townsend, 5th Mr Bert Stone, 8th Mr George Smith, 9th Mr George Ruddle, 11th Mr Bill Butler, 12th Mr Eric Wells, 13th Mr Tommy Cox, 14th Mr Percy Cox, 15th Mr Alf Turner, 17th Mr Joshua Main, 18th Mr Bill Hillier. Front row: 1st from the left Major Waterhouse, 6th Colonel Finch, 7th ? Nash, 8th ? Corbishley, 10th Mr Tommy Cox, 11th Mr Tom White. Many of these faces are probably indelibly etched on the memory of one local resident who recounts waking up one morning and peering into her parents' Stoke Row garden to see – to her horror and bewilderment, no doubt – strange movements in her father's Brussels sprouts patch. Investigations uncovered the Home Guard 'on manoeuvres' through the vegetables, with a camouflage of cabbage leaves on their helmets!

Water carriers. Mr William Wixen senior and Mr William Wixen junior, *c.* 1924. These gentlemen carried their water from the Maharajah's Well to their home three-quarters of a mile away. Piped water was not supplied to the whole village until 1950.

The Maharajah's Well. This was a gift to the people of Stoke Row from the Maharajah of Benares, who had been told of the deficiencies of water supply in the Chiltern hills. The well was officially opened on 24 May 1864 (also Queen Victoria's birthday) and use of the precious water was restricted to cooking and drinking.

This faded record, found in the long-empty well warden's cottage in 1976, shows the village schoolchildren outside the school in 1882, with their headmaster Mr Morris in the doorway. The occasion was a celebration of the survival by Queen Victoria of an assassination attempt. The festivities, provided by the generous Maharajah, included a dole of bread, tea or sugar, lunch at the Cherry Tree and tea for the schoolchildren.

Stoke Row chapel in the early part of this century. The extension to the chapel which gives it an altered appearance today, and provides a welcome kitchen and toilets, was built on in 1969.

The occasion of this gathering outside the chapel is not known, but the date must have been before 1882 since that was the year Mr James Giles (front row, holding a stick) died. James (born 1791) was the father of Mrs Eliza Cox (née Giles).

Interior of Stoke Row chapel. This picture shows the chapel some time in the early 1900s. Following refurbishment the interior has lighter coloured woodwork, and modern electrical fittings have replaced the lamps hung from chains seen here.

Vanishing homes. These cottages, near the Dog and Duck pub, Highmoor, were demolished in the mid-1960s and replaced by a modern pair. The photograph was taken around 1929 and shows, left to right: Mrs Jemima Webb, Mrs Dick Wells with baby Michael, Arthur Webb and Betty Webb.

Smallbones' Cottage, Newnham Hill. The above postcard has a postmark of 1905, and the picture below was probably taken some twenty years later. This cottage, too, has been demolished and replaced by a modern house.

Highmoor School on Witheridge Hill, which closed in the 1960s. Mr J.H. Baker, headmaster of Highmoor School for seventeen years from 1907, relates many tales of interest about the school on its 'island site' in his autobiography *School on the Ground Floor*, 1969/70. At Highmoor he was paid the grand sum of £70 a year, plus £15 for playing the church organ, while his wife, who was also his assistant at the school, received £50. Remarkably, in their first year they still managed to save £20!

School group, Highmoor, *c.* 1920. Notice the little boy on the right who has managed to sneak his teddy bear into the picture.

Witheridge Hill, looking up towards the school and the Rising Sun inn. The postmark on this postcard is 1921.

School play. These young ladies are shown in a play at Highmoor School, some time around 1920, and are, left to right: May Baker (daughter of the headmaster Mr J.H. Baker), Louisa and Ada Wells.

Tableau at Highmoor School, *c.* 1936. Standing, left: Margaret Stone; Madonna: Frances Cary; right: Kathleen Brakspear. Kneeling, left: Pam Springell; right: Lily Treadwell.

Madonna with angels. Frances Cary is again the Madonna. Margaret Stone is on the left, Lily Treadwell is on the right.

Living in the woods. Mr James Wise and his wife Becky, who lived in a house in the woods at Lower Highmoor in the latter part of the nineteenth century.

Ellen Turner and her sister, who lived in Highmoor Woods. Ellen was able to do ventriloquism and, by throwing her voice to other parts of the family's house, she convinced people – for a while – that it was haunted.

A charabanc outing from Highmoor, *c.* 1925. A good way to see some of the neighbouring areas to Stoke Row and Highmoor such as . . .

Greys Court. When this picture was taken Greys Court was privately owned. The attire of the figures on the left in front of the entrance suggests a turn-of-the-century date. In 1969 (the late) Sir Felix Brunner Bt gave Greys Court to the National Trust.

Crowsley Road, now Blounts Court Road, Peppard, possibly some time in the 1920s – although the view would have been much the same until the 1960s, except for improvements to the road surface.

Peppard School, on the north-east side of Peppard Common, around 1908–12. It no longer sports the flourishing creeper shown in this picture, but another one has grown on the right hand end of the building.

Two postcards of Peppard Common, looking west (above, postmark 1932) and east (below, postmark 1906). The first has a message in a child's writing: 'I have been sick all the night. I expect it is the change of air. Love Edie.' The card was being sent to 'Mum and all' at Shiplake Bottom. Not far to go for a change of air!

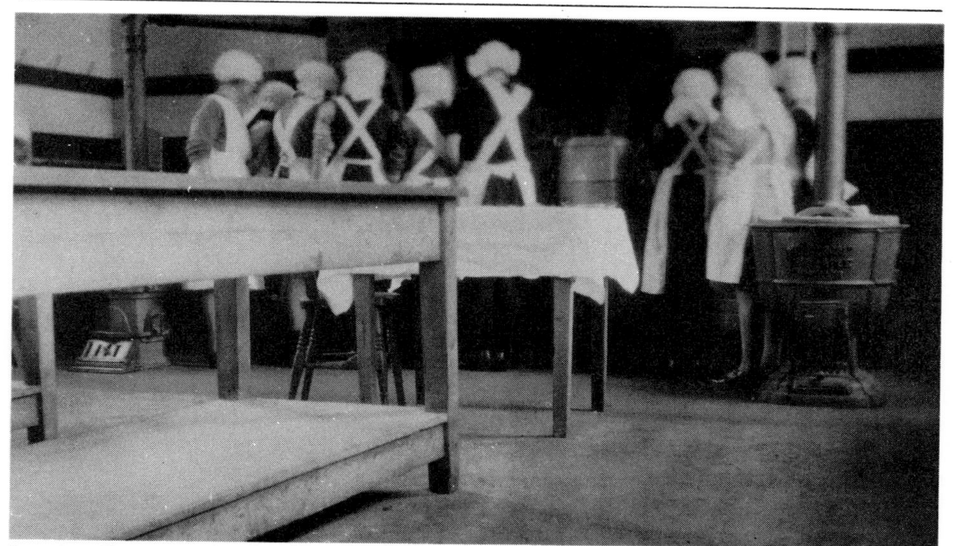

Sonning Common. A school domestic science class, 1930.

The village well (which is still there), near the church, Kidmore End, *c*. 1900. At this time only two or three houses at Kidmore End would have had indoor water, so the well was an important asset to the village – just as at Stoke Row. The carrier, seen stopped here, was also an important asset. For a shilling or two, he would deliver packages to Reading (or vice versa), and if there was room he would take a passenger.

School performers at Kidmore End School, *c.* 1914. The play in question was *Robin Hood, King of Sherwood*, the performance one to rival any at Highmoor School, no doubt.

SECTION SEVEN

Around Nettlebed

Nettlebed is situated some 700 ft up in Chiltern beechwood country at the junction of four main roads: to Henley, Reading, Thame and Oxford. In the eighteenth century its High Street saw many a stage coach, and its inns offered hospitality to many a weary traveller. Although the Red Lion and Bull might have closed, the general aspect of the High Street appears hardly to have changed.

Nettlebed was also renowned as a brick-making centre: tiles and bricks have been made at Nettlebed since the Middle Ages. It is recorded that 35,000 tiles were made there for Wallingford Castle in 1365, and in 1416/17 Thomas Stonor paid Michael Warwick £40 for making 200,000 'brykes' at his kiln in Crocker End, near Nettlebed. These were conveyed – for a further payment of £15 – to Stonor House, three miles distant. By the middle of the nineteenth century Nettlebed would have presented a flourishing industrial scene of clay pits, waterpools and brickyards. But by the middle of the twentieth century the scale and nature of the industry had changed so much that the modest Nettlebed kilns had become defunct. The only surviving kiln, last used in 1938, now stands somewhat incongruously among modern houses at the entrance to the village.

It is in the nature of man never to be satisfied, and this is borne out by a favourite old tale from Nettlebed, relating to the splendid views it offered of the surrounding countryside, particularly from Windmill Hill, the highest point on the Chilterns in this area. Not content to stand and gaze, one man called Jarvis sought artificial means to increase his field of vision, and asked to be tied to the sails of the windmill which stood on the hill until 1912. When he was hoisted aloft, however, he became so giddy that he had to be brought back down.

There is a legend, too, about Nell Gwynn staying at Soundess on the edge of Nettlebed from where she could see Windsor Castle (the view is now obscured by trees). It is said that if Charles II was coming to see her someone at the castle would light a fire. When Nell saw the smoke she would know she should prepare herself to receive the King – and possibly get rid of any other visiting suitors before he arrived! The story is without foundation, of course, although Charles did bring Nell to the area on more than one occasion.

The selection of pictures takes us through Nettlebed to the surrounding woodland, to Joyce Grove (once the home of author and explorer Peter Fleming and his brother Ian, creator of James Bond), to Nettlebed's largest hamlet, Crocker End, and on an excursion to Huntercombe Golf Club and Nuffield Place.

High Street, Nettlebed, with the Red Lion Hotel, around the turn of the century. Nettlebed High Street today remains remarkably similar to the view in this old postcard, although the building on the right closest to the camera has gone and the Red Lion is a private house. The best known story about the Red Lion is one that bears testimony to the hospitable welcome it extended to travellers of every kind. In the summer of 1782 a young Prussian, Pastor Carl Philipp Moritz, was making a tour of England. Travelling on foot, however, he found to his dismay that innkeepers, while being most welcoming towards carriage folk, treated him with suspicion. In fact, when he came to Henley he decided not even to try his luck at one of the inns because they all looked too grand for him. Nettlebed's Red Lion seemed less forbidding, and indeed, to his surprise, he was given 'a carpeted bedroom and a very good bed', even though he had not arrived in any style. The next day, a Sunday, the landlord Mr Illing even loaned him his family Prayer Book, as Moritz decided to attend church. This he enjoyed so much that he went again in the afternoon. After that he had great difficulty in leaving Nettlebed at all, so enchanted was he by the village. He set off three times and returned three times before he could tear himself away from his 'favourite Nettlebed'.

The Myrtles, High Street, a card postmarked 1905. Nothing covers the Myrtles' brick frontage today and its railings have gone, but otherwise it has changed little. Mr John Godwin (born in 1914, and whose family has lived in Nettlebed since at least the 1600s) recalls that his sisters Lily and Bertha went to school cookery lessons here from around 1910 and 1914. Local WI records note that the Domestic Science Centre opened at the Myrtles in 1909 and classes continued to be held there for approximately twenty years. Girls aged ten years and above attended the classes from the Church School (now the Church Hall).

The Bull Hotel, High Street, a card postmarked 1907. The Bull Hotel closed recently, and the hairdressers next to it in this view closed some ten years ago.

The Strange sisters, Carrie and Anne, known sometimes as the 'Dutch Dolls' because they dressed similarly. These ladies, with their perambulator and stout walking sticks, were a familiar sight on the roads around Nettlebed in the early years of this century. They were the daughters of Nettlebed's blacksmith and lived in Forge Cottage, near Wanbourne Pond. When their father died, so one story goes, they bought a perambulator and set up a shopping service for neighbours, in order to earn a living. They regularly walked from Nettlebed to Wallingford or Henley. Any money they received was promptly buried in their garden, because they did not trust banks, and it was only when they died that their secret treasure was discovered.

Nettlebed windmill originally stood near Watlington but was carried section by section to Nettlebed in 1826. It burned down in 1912. Many believe the fire was not entirely unwelcome to the owner. These pictures show the windmill before and after the 'disaster'.

Church parade past Pottery Yard on the coronation day of King George VI in 1937. Nettlebed's kiln can be seen in the background. The parade is led by Mr Martin Beasley, with Mr Dennis Clarke (drum) and Mr Reg Sparrowhawk (cymbals) following.

Watlington Street around the turn of the century, showing Wanbourne Pond on the right. The pond has since been filled in and a children's playing area created.

Halfridge Woods, as tranquil today as in this early picture.

Joyce Grove was built in 1904 by Robert Fleming on the site of an older house. In 1913 it was struck by lightning, and during repair work a new wing was added. There was another fire in the 1930s. In 1940 the Flemings gave the mansion to St Mary's Hospital, London, and it was used as a Preliminary Training School for nurses and then a convalescent home. It is now, of course, a Sue Ryder home. This picture shows furniture being rescued after the 1913 fire.

Crocker End has hardly changed at all this century, as these two early postcards show.

Huntercombe Golf Club: some early players. Huntercombe Golf Club was established in 1900/1 and for sixty-three years was owned by a proprietor, most notably (from 1925 to 1963) W.R. Morris, later Viscount Nuffield. Since 1963 it has been a members' club, operated as a limited company.

Huntercombe golf links. From the early years the club provided transport – not always reliable – to and from Henley station for its members. This picture shows a bus supplied in 1909 by the Maudslay Motor Company.

Kathleen Francis, a maid at Nuffield Place, seen here in the garden with Lord Nuffield's scotties. The picture was taken during the 1930s. Mr William Richard Morris, founder of Morris Motors, made Nuffield Place his home in 1933, and he took his title of Lord Nuffield from the village. Nuffield Place was bequeathed to Nuffield College, Oxford on his death in 1963, and it is now open to the public on certain days. Built in 1914 and enlarged in 1933, it survives as a rare example of a complete upper-middle-class home of the 1930s.

SECTION EIGHT

Mapledurham to Goring

A boat journey from Mapledurham to Goring and Streatley will provide the traveller with some of the most beautiful riverside scenes along the Thames and some charming stopping points.

At Mapledurham there is the Thames' oldest working watermill and the fine sixteenth-century Mapledurham House. There is also the nearby flint parish church of St Margaret, whose most famous rector was Lord Augustus Fitz-Clarence, the fifth of William IV's ten children by his mistress, the actress Mrs Jordan. Whitchurch's attractive brick-and-flint houses seem caught in a time capsule, and it is easy to appreciate why the village was a favourite gathering place for the social set during those halcyon Edwardian summers – at least one imagines them thus – when the cult of the Thames was at its peak. Goring and Streatley, too, still breathe the rarefied air of a genteel age, although sadly some of the finest of their houses have been demolished this century, and modern traffic has brought problems of congestion.

Goring and Streatley, like so many near-neighbours, are interesting rivals. Here the Thames divides Oxfordshire (and Goring) from Berkshire (and Streatley), and during past centuries there seems to have been little rapport between the two villages. Such a divide between the two communities is not the case today, though. The local history society, which helps to preserve such historical anecdotes, combines Goring and Streatley, and this year the Goring and Streatley Regatta was revived after nearly eighty years in abeyance.

Some of the villages' shops are vanishing, but the local railway station, situated in Goring, still serves the two communities. As Jerome K. Jerome noted when weighing the relative merits of the two villages in *Three Men in a Boat*: 'Goring is not nearly so pretty a little spot to stop at as Streatley, if you have your choice; but it is passing fair enough in its way, and is nearer the railway in case you want to slip off without paying your hotel bill.' Luckily, most of the renowned inns, such as the Bull (favoured by the three men in the boat) and the Swan, both at Streatley, the Old Leatherne Bottel near South Stoke, and the Miller of Mansfield at Goring, have survived any such anti-social behaviour!

This section follows the river from Mapledurham to Goring, with a small inland excursion to Goring Heath and Woodcote.

Mapledurham Mill, *c.* 1910. Restoration work on the mill was completed in 1978 and it is now the oldest working watermill on the Thames.

The old weir and cottage at Mapledurham, *c.* 1865. The weir seen at Mapledurham today has been completely remodelled in concrete and steel, and the cottage has vanished.

Mapledurham House, *c.* 1890. Sir Michael Blount, Lieutenant of the Tower of London, built Mapledurham House in 1588, and it has remained the property of the Blount family and their descendants, the Eystons. It is open to the public in the summer. The poet Alexander Pope was among visitors to the house in the early eighteenth century, when he seems to have been an admirer of both Blount daughters, Teresa and Martha. He wrote of Teresa, who had 'retired' from London in 1714 and gone to Mapledurham: 'She went to plain work, and to purling brooks, Old fashioned halls, dull aunts and croaking rooks, She went from opera, park, assembly, play, To morning walks, and prayers three hours a day.' Another poet struck by the attractive sisters was John Gay, who remarked 'I see two lovely sisters, hand in hand, the fair-haired Martha and Teresa brown.'

Hardwick House, the late-Tudor mansion built by the Lybbe family is seen here from the river in around 1900. Queen Elizabeth is said to have once stayed here as the guest of Richard Lybbe, and Charles I was also entertained at Hardwick when he was a prisoner at Caversham.

The Warren Scout troop was also entertained at Hardwick, when its members enjoyed a tea party there in 1910.

Whitchurch: the church of St Mary the Virgin and the mill seen across the river, *c.* 1887. On the right is the ferryman's cottage. The long line of dazzling white washing in the garden is the result of the ferryman's wife carrying on a flourishing laundry business. The small building on the right was the laundry house.

'The end of the Pang, at Pangbourne Wharf, where it runneth into the Thames – with the old Whitchurch Bridge in the distance' is the undated, handwritten message which accompanies this picture. Today, the elms have gone from this view.

The toll-gate keeper at Whitchurch, *c.* 1900. The toll-bridge across the Thames between Whitchurch and Pangbourne was built following an Act of Parliament in 1792.

The Greyhound Inn, High Street, *c.* 1887. The Greyhound building has since been extended by a few feet towards the forge (on the left), now The Old Forge, which has had its roof altered and a bay window added downstairs.

The Bridge House (*c.* 1875) is now called the Ferry Boat and looks considerably different to how it did when this picture was taken. There has been an extension to the side of the pub nearest the camera and the building is now painted white. The fence has gone, opening up space for the present car park.

Woodcote church, dedicated to St Leonard, was built in Victorian times. This picture shows the church around 1844.

The Village Hall, Woodcote, 1920s. Except for an extension built onto the end of the hall closest to the camera and obvious changes such as the introduction of road markings and the removal of the telegraph pole, this scene remains virtually unaltered.

Almshouses, St Bartholomew's chapel and a primary school at Goring Heath were built and endowed by the will of Mr Henry Alnut in 1724. The school (above, *c.* 1910) opened officially in May 1989 as further almshouses. The view below (*c.* 1890), which shows the school and original almshouses behind, is obscured today by trees.

A view over Goring, *c.* 1888, taken from the church tower and looking towards the Streatley hills. In the foreground is the old Goring and Streatley toll-bridge which was built in 1837. By 1910 it was known to be unsafe, but due to lack of funds (and the First World War) it was not replaced by a new bridge until 1923. In that year tolls to cross the bridge were abolished.

St Thomas' church, Goring viewed from across the river, *c.* 1875. The original church was built in the eleventh century by Robert D'Oyley, although it has undergone many changes since. In 1898, after this picture was taken, a rounded apse was added following excavations which revealed the line of the former Norman apse pulled down in the Middle Ages.

Cleeve Lock, *c.* 1890. The keeper's cottage at Cleeve Lock is one of the oldest on the river, and this picture certainly lives up to the opinion Jerome K. Jerome expressed in *Three Men in a Boat* that 'They are picturesque little spots, these locks. The stout old lock-keeper, or his cheerful-looking wife, or bright-eyed daughter, are pleasant folk to have a passing chat with. . . The Thames would not be the fairyland it is without flower-decked locks.' He did, however, add a wry aside that, increasingly, the benign old lock-keeper was being superseded by 'excitable, nervous old men quite unfitted for their post'! The original Cleeve pound lock was built in 1797, replacing a sixteenth-century flash lock. In 1874 it was rebuilt using stone instead of timber and since then it has been mechanized and improved further.

The rebuilding of Goring Lock, 1922. There was a flash lock at Goring, as at Cleeve, in the sixteenth century. The name derived from the flush, or flash of water created when sluice gates opened to allow a boat to pass. They could be the cause of floods, and the later pound locks, which transferred boats gently through their 'cistern' from one level of water to another, were more satisfactory. Goring pound lock was built using timber in 1797 and rebuilt with stone in 1922. Like Cleeve, it is now mechanized. Goring flash lock had been the scene of the great tragedy in 1674 when sixty people ('and one mare' according to one account) were drowned. They were returning from Goring Feast, thought to have been a sort of fair or revels, to Streatley, but rowed too close to the weir as they passed through the lock. When the 'Sad and Deplorable News' was published it was accompanied by the following caveat:

> Readers, this story is both strange and true
> And for your good presented unto you.
> Be careful of your life all sins to fly,
> Lest you by death be taken suddenly.
> When he is sent on you arrest to make
> No Fees, nor Bail, can purchase your escape.

Many said that it served the revellers right for going to Goring, such was the rivalry between the two communities.

Two riverside inns. The Swan, Streatley (shown above at the turn of the century) has been an inn since at least the seventeenth century, when it was under a bargee's licence. In the twentieth century it has been much altered and is now a hotel. The Leatherne Bottel near South Stoke (below, *c.* 1873) was renowned in the seventeenth and eighteenth centuries for its spring whose waters were reputed to cure ills such as skin diseases and eye complaints. The Leatherne Bottel, along with other inns owned by the local Gundry Brewery, was bought by Brakspear's in 1940/1.

Station Road, Goring around the turn of the century. Only superficial changes, such as loss of thatch and alterations to fencing, make this view different from that of today.

Railway staff at Goring station, *c.* 1900.

Goring station shortly after 1892/3, when its broad-gauge tracks were removed and four new tracks built. The railway came to Goring in 1840 and in the late nineteenth century was largely responsible for increasing the local population: it offered the wealthy businessman the chance to live in an attractive riverside setting and to commute quite easily to work in London. Many fine houses were built at this time. It is notable, however, that Streatley was less affected than Goring, and one can only surmise that this was partly because the station was built on the Oxfordshire side of the 'divide'.

Nun's Acre in a picture believed to date from the 1950s. Nun's Acre, on the west side of Cleeve Road, was one of the large houses which gave Goring its grand and genteel atmosphere. It was demolished in 1967 and the site developed into Nun's Acre Estate.

Edwardians at leisure. This teatime scene on the lawn of The Temple, a grand nineteenth-century house at the end of the Cleeve Road, epitomizes the life of the gentry. The Temple was owned at the time by Mr and Mrs Telford Simpson, who are the gentleman and lady sitting on the extreme right of the picture. The date is 1908. Sadly, the house was demolished in 1930.

The Goring and Streatley Regatta, founded by the Telford Simpson family, was one of the biggest regattas on the Thames from 1887 until it ceased in 1914. The course ran from the Beetle and Wedge at Moulsford to Cleeve Lock. The Regatta was revived in July 1992.

Some watched in style in the committee barge (above); others watched from the bank (below). The race in progress is a dongola race, with men and women competing together. One would think that the women – attired so elegantly in their long skirts – would find it difficult to keep pace with the men.

Challenge Pairs Final. The steam from the umpire's launch suggests it was struggling to keep up! But it would have offered a welcome rescue vessel to the 'damsels in distress' recorded in Jerome K. Jerome's account of a notable regatta incident in his autobiography *My Life and Times*. 'Goring Regatta was always good fun when Frank Benson, the actor [who lived at Goring], stage-managed it,' but 'one year, his ambition ran away with him.' The aquatic drama he dreamed up, which involved a group of damsels being 'rescued' by canoe in the quickest possible time from an island in mid-stream, ended at the first attempt with gallant rescuer and dainty damsel rather wet and bedraggled. 'The remaining four ladies elected to be rescued by the umpire's launch.'

Acknowledgements

The compilation of this book has only been possible because of the great help I have received from other people. I should like to extend my thanks to everyone who has provided photographs, postcards and information. If I have omitted the name of anyone to whom I owe thanks I ask them to accept my apologies. I also accept responsibility for any mistakes which might have crept into the text. Recollections of dates, people and places are not always as exact as one might hope, but in the final text I have taken the decision to include or omit such information.

My gratitude to the Oxfordshire Photographic Archive in the Centre for Oxfordshire Studies and to the *Henley Standard* has already been mentioned. Additionally, I should like to give special thanks to Dr Malcolm Graham, Head of the Centre for Oxfordshire Studies, for his advice, to Mrs Nuala la Vertue for the hours she spent searching out the pictures I selected from the Archive, and to Mr George Tuckfield, editor of the *Henley Standard* for his readiness to promote my research.

Where space has permitted and the captions have allowed, I have mentioned the sources of photographs in the pages of the book. Other contributors deserve equal acknowledgement and the full list of those who have combined to help create this book is: Mrs Mary Adams; Mr and Mrs A. Austin; Mr P.W. Brakspear; Mrs Avril Bryant; Miss Mary Burge; Mr George Bushell; Mrs Dorothy Booth; Mr John Crocker; Mr K.P. Fisher; Mr A. Fordham; Mr Stan Gardiner; Mr R.S. Goddard, Secretary, Henley Royal Regatta; Mr John Godwin; Mr Cyril Mather; Mr William Neal; Mrs Florence Povey; Miss Sybil Reeves; Mr and Mrs A. Simpson and the Goring and Streatley Local History Society; Mr Bill Smith and the residents of Remenham Place; Mrs Angela Spencer-Harper; Mr Peter Sutherland; Miss Dorothy Walman; Mrs Laureen Williamson; Miss Valerie Wootton.